Internet Marketing for Seniors

from Concept to Delivery

Published by LuLu Publishing
First published in USA 2007

ISBN: 978-1-4357-0587-6

Email the author at tmyapterry@gmail.com
    or at his website at www.AirCoast.com

Contents

This book is dedicated to my parents, my brothers, sisters, nephews, niece and also my many business associates.

Author: Yap Tat Meng

Prologue

From farmers to college kids, everyone is jumping in to get a piece of the growing Internet Marketing cake. It is no wonder because the internet is the only way for each and every one of us to 'put' our voice out there and to be counted. No matter what you want to do, you can achieve it there. There are more than eighty million (end 2006) websites and six billion web pages have been identified by the search engines. Daily, there are ten thousand new websites added with the registrars and there are many more billions of pages that are yet to be found by the search engines. What does all this mean?

It simply means people will do most of their things on the net. Today, if people can figure up a way to do something, their first thought is to go to the net and see how to fit the thing in. It also means that if you want to make a statement (any statement), you will also have to go on the net. Are you missing something here? You should also be grabbing yourself a piece of the cake, if you are not already involved. I am talking about 'Internet Marketing' and I would like to define it as the method of seeking a market for your product (or anything else) through the internet.

It used to be true that when we talk of the net, we usually refer to a bunch of fresh college kids fiddling with their laptops trying to send some very important message to others while munching their buggers and seeping latte. Today, it is no longer true as a whole lot of other guys and gals are also getting connected, though not necessary for the same reasons. As the mad rush to embrace the internet begun around 1997, one sector of the population, in particular, the seniors, and those approaching retirement were somehow left out. This is due mainly to their own attitudes (technophobia) and also because there were barriers to learn new technologies. As a result, these groups have to feel contented just looking eagerly by, and at times had pretended that they could not be bothered as to whether the internet existed or not. However, as net activities increased many folds, the elderly could not remain unperturbed any more. For one thing, retirement means having a lot of spare time (and cash as well) and nothing else to do. For another, most governments have instituted programs to encourage this sector (growing fast) to embrace the internet, so that the seniors (with their experiences) can become again a useful part of society. No one wants to be left out, right? As a group, the seniors, especially baby boomers (about seventy million in the US alone) still have a lot to contribute to the society. They have the experience, energy, time and the money to make things happen. Unfortunately, they lack many information technology skills, especially in such areas like ecommerce and networking. Sensing such a void, it is my intention to illuminate these groups with a practical discourse on Internet Marketing. I am a baby boomer myself, and I have successfully used Internet Marketing to sell my own designed product and establishing my own brand at the same time. I did it from idea conception to final delivery. It was a great learning curve for me, and I am sure it would be a fantastic and exciting journey for you as well. Along the way, you will surely encounter many new problems, but when you learn to overcome it, like what I did, you will have that great feeling of satisfaction that money cannot buy. I will lead you into this treasure trove. You will also feel exhilarated and look younger (at least in heart) because you can also do what those college kids have been doing! I know you will enjoy this journey, and hopefully you will achieve success and even write about it to serve as a legacy for your children. You will be able to say "Yes, Grandpa (or Grandma) has been there before" to your grand children.

Today, you can do many things using the net, but its main function remained as a medium of communication. So if you have something to tell to the world (yes, it is a globalized audience), you can either whisper or shout it loud through a website, a blog or through a social network. There are many people out there who wished to learn about how to improve their lives, be it in a social or commercial nature. My intention of writing this book is to help them to better grasp the finer points of Internet Marketing, a subject that is on the minds of many people. You can of course find many Internet Marketing books in the market, but this book is written especially for those of a matured age and who had just started on the internet journey. It is also written from a viewpoint of a matured person, who had forced himself to learn about using computers (at age 50) just so that he can complete his life long vision of selling his own brand of product. That is me of course and I believed that there are many out there who also harbored the same aspiration. I did it with very little help from others. My budget was just five thousand bucks and with plenty of creativeness and resourcefulness, I managed to not only sell my own designed and patented products, but also established my own brand. I will now impart that know-how to you, hoping that you will be able to join my club of lonely doers. In order to fully grasp the practical aspects of Internet Marketing, the reader should at least have some basic internet surfing skills; otherwise they will not be able to understand fully what this book teaches. If you are a complete newbie to the internet, I would advise you to at least attend some practical internet surfing courses before reading further. Or you can ask your junior to help. Better still get them into the Internet Marketing wagon for they usually have loads of ideas. Although this book is written for the mature dad and moms out there, it will also be appropriate for those who wished to turn their websites into a great marketing vehicle that they can be proud of. Take Internet Marketing as a journey, an exciting journey, but do not measure your success only in monetary terms as it might come in other forms, many of which is hard to measure. When you have followed the advices that are described in this book, you would inevitably taste success, first in small measures and later, hopefully in torrents. Before you continue reading, I would like to qualify my statement that "Internet Marketing, being part of an evolving technology, will see changes all the time and those who partake in it will need vision and creativeness to stay above the curve".

How pervasive is the internet?

Just look around you and you can see how pervasive the internet is. You have people booking their tour tickets, filing their tax returns, emailing their buddies half a world away, all through their cell phones. However, Internet Marketing, or the offering of products and services through the internet is a huge ball game, and you can be easily mislead by all the hypes that are thrown at it. For example, there are experts out there who can guarantee that you will make your millions by just putting in two weeks of 'hard work' and making your website flooded with people eager to buy your products! So on and on it goes, for the most gullible of course.

Exactly what is achievable for the small guy is mired in deceits and unsubstantiated facts. Amidst all the hypes, there are indeed many cases of successes out there, both small and big. Success may also mean different things to different people, but generally people could be considered successful if they manage to achieved part of the goal that they set out to achieve, be it in monetary terms or otherwise. Then again, there might be other goals for internet marketing, like stamping out a brand presence for later intentions. There is also the benefit of market testing through the internet before a full marketing program is launched. In short, Internet Marketing can help you to do many things, but you have to learn it as there are not many out there who have successfully dabbled with it before. There are plenty of them who gave up as well, but don't let their negative comments dissuade you. Whatever aim that you have, only one thing is for sure, and that is Internet Marketing is for those who are serious and are determined to slog it out. There are basically two types of Internet Marketing. One is the marketing of products and services from producer to consumer (b2c) and the other is from producer to producer (b2b). If you don't belonged to this group of people, then my best advice is for you to stop reading here. This course is not suitable for you then. I am writing this book as a person who had gone through all the various processes and I believed that my experiences will be beneficial to you in someway or other. For myself, I would consider as successful as to what I have achieved so far, and along the way, I have managed to sell a range of products that I have personally conceived, patented, made and also established a brand for it. And all these on a tiny weenie budget of five thousand dollars only! If you shared my vision, then read on as you will gain tremendously from the pointers that I will write about. Wish you great success.

Chapter 1

What can I sell?

This is the starter and the most important question that only you can answer. It is so important that if you are not sure of what you can sell, you should stop thinking of doing internet marketing until you do. It is also one of the toughest questions that anyone has to answer! But you heard it somewhere that if you don't have your own product, you can always sell someone else's product, right? Yes, of course you can, but what are you missing then? Plenty, no doubt about it and I will tell you now before anything else.

Firstly,
When you sell your own product, you are in almost total control. And isn't that what you want in the first place, bear in mind that Internet Marketing is a long term game plan, nothing short of ten years of your life blood! If you think you will only give it a try of six months, then don't go anywhere near it, but if you have that burning desire to prove to the world, then pull out all the stops and embrace it.

Secondly,
Your product means 'Your Brand'. The meaning of this is that supposing you are going to sell your own brand of soft drink, you should not touch anymore 'Cola' or 'Sprite' or '100 Plus'. Not only that, wherever you go, you will have to flip out that brand bottle of yours, as well as telling the whole world that they should also try your brand! Yes, maybe it is a bit

mercenary here, but that is the difference between selling your own product and selling someone else's product.

Thirdly,
Every exposure that your product has goes a long way to increasing its brand value. Think of antiques, the older it gets, the more valuable it becomes. It also goes the same for other people's brand, the more people selling it, the more exposures it get, so it becomes more valuable, but the value benefits someone else's, not you, although you had put in the effort. Why go and sell other people's product then?

Fourthly,
With your own brand, you can now get others to sell it for you. You can then use affiliates or franchise programs to expand it worldwide. Think of it as a cunningly slavish scheme where you are the master and those other guys out there as slaves!

Fifth,
If you have a successful brand, your trademark can be sold off for a tidy sum of money. If however your brand doesn't make it to the top, it can still be sold off for monetary gains, albeit for a lesser sum. If someone were to perceive your brand as suitable for their purpose, they might buy it from you for a tidy sum even though it might not be a successful brand. Beauty is in the eyes of the beholder as the saying goes, so coming up with a fortuitous name is worth your time. Some names rhyme with certain products, but because names are a limited commodity (at least on the internet); it is much easier to buy it from the market.

Sixth,

Building a brand is the stuff of empire builders, a trait that we normally don't see in people having it these days. For these rare breeds, the internet has given them an opportunity to showcase their talents and making it big. And even though you may not be sure whether you have what it takes to be one, do give yourself a chance, won't you? Were you born a century earlier, you would not have this opportunity!

Now that I have told you all the good reasons why you should start with your own product, we will proceed to our next task, and that is to determine whether you can come up with your own product. Can you? "Not sure, never done that before". Ah, this is the big question, and a big hurdle, right? You would have noticed that I mentioned all those good reasons why you should have your own products first, before you have a chance to jump in and grab someone else's product and do an affiliates selling. Why not, everybody is doing it? But do you know that at least 95% of those doing affiliate programs don't succeed. And the other 5% though making good money is not sure whether they should spent the rest of their lives promoting products that they don't own! So let us sit down and see what you can do if you don't go the affiliates way. Say good bye to it if possible, chuck out the 'me too' type of syndrome and do something you will be proud of, and your children will be proud of.

Product ideas

Let us be down to earth. Consider this. Not every product is suitable for Internet Marketing. Here are things to consider before you jump in

1) Tangible products that have weight should be considered only if its monetary value is high compared to its shipping cost (either locally or overseas). Example: Wooden carvings costing upwards of $350.

2) Tangible products that have a large volume compared to its monetary value should not be considered as well because shipping cost will also take into consideration the volume. Example: Pillows and blankets

3) Tangible products that have liquid contents and cost very little is a no no. Example: Orange squash.

4) Expensive items must be insurable, otherwise it is no go. Example: Jewelry.

5) Products with contents that is volatile and bottled in glass should not be considered as it could not stand rough handling whilst being shipped. Example: Brandy.

6) Cheap articles that come in various sizes should not be considered as there is a high proportion of it being returned for exchange. Example: Sandals

7) Products that cannot withstand being dropped must not be considered. Example: Computer Monitors.

8) Products that can be banned or restricted from importation in the receiving countries should not be considered. Example: Imitation firearms.

9) Products that have copy right restrictions should not be considered. Examples: VCD and DVD

10) Medicines that are subjected to patent rights in importing countries where disputes might arise.

11) Live animals that requires quarantines.

So you can see that not everything is suitable as far as ecommerce is concerned, but if you are not sure, go over to your shipping company to enquire about the shipping charges first. Before you send any goods out of your country go to the foreign embassy to enquire about trade matters in the importing country first as different countries have different laws.

Chapter 2

Conceiving your idea

Ideation, or the conceiving of ideas is a very tough nut to crack, but it is easier if you do it in small little steps. You will need inspiration, concentration and some rare moments to yourself (like in your bath room), and also a determination to never give up. But you have never done it before, right? Wrong! You have definitely, in your past thought about something interesting, but at that time there was no need to pursue it further, so you had conveniently forgotten about it. Think again, go back some years and you might remember something. The idea, no matter how silly you might think will form your seed idea. Take it out of the fridge, roll it around, toss it a few turns and loft and behold, you now have a good idea on your hands! Sounds very easy, right? Believe me, it is not that difficult, I have done it many times. If you need some inspirations, how about getting for yourself a book that I had written entitled "Inventing: The moment before the spark came". This book will teach you about being inventive and put your mind in a better position to be creative. It might just spark that idea of yours that had all the time resided in your mind. The book is available on-line at LuLu, Amazon and BarnsandNoble. The book's ISBN: 978-1-4303-1304-5.

Looking back

A lot of new ideas are actually derived from previous ideas, so the place to start is just go and pick anything and role play with it. For example, supposing you have picked a wooden chair, so just think of how you can add other features to it to make it into something else.

All right, how about this. I am sure you have seen many of those exercising equipments available at the shopping mall. You have peddles, rollers, belts and other spring tensioners on these health machines, some of it even looked like moon rovers. And of course it cost a bomb. Now take another look at the chair that you have picked. Chairs normally come with a back rest. Just imagine, supposing your chair rest now has a hollow inside, and you can attach some spring mounted belts that has a handle which rest on the sides of the chair rest. Now, when you sit down on the chair, you can use your hands to grab the handle, pull it out, relax, then pull it again, just like when you are pulling those exercising belts of exercising machines. What you have is a chair with an exercising belt built in so that you can flex your arm muscles when you are bored. You can of course use both your arms. Do you have this kind of chair in the market yet? This is just an example of a product that is a combination of two existing products. When you combine the two items, you get a new product. It need not stop here of course, and it can take other forms.

This is how ideas are sparked, and you can pick anything for a start and roll it into something else. The ideas are in fact just right in front of your eyes, in your near surroundings, but you need to train your mind to see it. The techniques are discussed in my invention book, so after trying and you still can't come out with any viable idea, go and grab the book and spark your thoughts for a more exciting life.

When you have finally conceived your idea, you will need to find out whether the idea that you have is not available in the market yet. You might find some similarities along the way. Don't be dishearten yet, as you can still tweak it and turn it into something that is unique and without comparison. This will probably be a long journey, but be determined and you will finally be rewarded. Your next step is to build a prototype and test it. For those of you who are not technically inclined, you can rope in someone else who can help out.

As you are already aware of, intangible products like digital software programs lends itself best to internet marketing. Whilst tangible products can also be marketed through the internet, there are certain considerations to be taken into account. The most obvious one is the profit margin of the product where when you take into consideration the shipping charges (the cost of delivery), your packaging cost, returns cost, pilferage cost and others that might eat into your mark ups. As most items are charged according to their weight, a product of low value but high weight (or volume) ratio will not be suitable for Internet Marketing. It would even be more critical if you have to do international shipping, so take time to evaluate the viability of your chosen product before proceeding further. The other thing that is of importance is the returns issue, where your product might have to be sent back because of either wrong size issue or color schemes.

When your product is subjected to these vagaries, you should take it into account on your product price. If yours is a unique product and having little competition, then you are on a much better ground. Which reminds me to stress that having a unique proposition is an important consideration before you plunge into Internet Marketing. However, it is not an everyday affair that you can churn out a unique product, so have plenty of patience to figure out one is more important than selling a product that is a dime a dozen. One thing that you should never do is to rush into anything because blindly following what everyone else is doing is a sure way to be stuck in quick sand later on.

Can I afford the time and money?

The next question that you have to tackle is do you have the time and money to pursue this Internet Marketing thing, assuming that you have already narrowed down the possibilities?

Time factor
Like most people who are considering internet marketing, you already have an existing job. In order to undertake a new project, you will probably have to apportion much of your time to it. Most internet marketers started of doing it part time first, then fulltime when the income stabilizes. When there is some sort of manufacturing involved, then you need to spend more time with it. A full fledge internet marketing business will need all your available time, so before stepping into one, be prepared to give up your previous job, whatever it is.

Money factor
Money is always the most critical factor as no amount of it is ever enough. Also, most projects failed because funds run out too fast before sufficient profits come in. As in any enterprise, there is always the issue of unexpected

expenses cropping up here and there. Having a contingency plan just in case unexpected problems crop up is a good idea.

Who to sell to

An important part of the research that you will have to do is to identify who would most likely buy your product. It is very important to first identify the right group of buyers or to locate where your prospective buyers are. I know this is a difficult question to answer, but you will have to do your best to identify it. Say you are going hunting and you have only a limited number of ammunitions. Like most everybody, your resources is limited, so every shot counts. When you correctly identify your buyers, then your resources will stretch further, and your chance of succeeding is greater.

You have to do your research in identifying your prospects. If yours is a computer program, identifying your market is very much easier. When you have a tangible product, the first place to go is to ask around, especially those people in the trade. Shopping malls might also be an appropriate place as there are many products there to check on. The next place is of course the Internet. Your main concern is the competition and products that are competing in the same range. Have a good grasp of the retailing prices as this will help you in how much to mark up your price.

After having identified your most likely buyers and where they will come from, you will be better equipped to do your copy writing. Remember, what you write on your web site and your catalogues will make or break you. There is also a distinct difference between on-line and off-line buyers. If you were knowledgeable in the brick and mortar market, do not assume that the on-line market will have the same demographics and characteristics. Additionally, the on-line market, which encompasses the global region will response quite differently. If funds are available, it would be wise to conduct some strategic market surveys at different countries if your intended market is spread out. However, market surveys don't paint an accurate picture, and it should only be taken as a help.

As an entrepreneur, you will have to rely on some 'gut feeling' to identify your market sector. Fortunately, the internet allows you a low cost testing platform. And the vehicle to use is the so called 'pay per click (more commonly known as PPC program). You can use the PPC program to advertise your product on the internet and get very good response feedback. With this method, you are actually putting up your product to a much targeted set of consumers and when you receive enquiries, you will be able to judge for yourself whether there are indeed buyers out there. In most likelihood, you will have to adjust the quality, packaging and cost of your product, at least for the on-line buyers.

In cases of an entirely new product (something that has never been seen before) range, you will most likely be overwhelmed with loads of questions, some of which you would never have imagined before. I have many times being astounded by the way people ask their questions, some of it seems illogical at first, but later make sense. In this respect, big and established corporations should use PPC exercises to better gauge the offering of their new products. It is a fast, effective means to market testing not available with conventional marketing regimes. Just imagine, search engine giant Google derives half its annual revenue from PPC advertisers! This is the money that is driving the internet now! If you use PPC methods to do market testing, you will definitely find out some short comings of your initial offer. Perhaps your price or your quality might not be right. You will have to move very fast to tackle these short comings. But if you find that it is not possible, then you will have to offer an improved version. You really need to have a plan 'b' or even a plan 'c'.

How to sell

Once you have determined what and who you are going to sell your product to, the next question is to sort out the delivery and the payment system. Depending on the nature of your product, you will have to determine an appropriate delivery system. There are many successful examples found on the net, so identifying one to use is not a problem. However, not every product is the same as there are different sets of conditions for different places. What may work for some might not work for you!

Assuming that you are selling to end users, some of the methods available are:-

i) Sell from your website to the consumers and ship from there.
ii) Sell from your website, but ship from one of your on-line sub-agents located nearest your buyer. This is a more cost efficient method if you have a globalized market.

iii) Direct all orders and shipping to your nearest dealers (your franchisees).

Financing

After you have come up with a viable concept, you will have to evaluate and see whether you have enough money to finance it for at least two years running. If you are a first timer entrepreneur, it would be advisable to consult someone else who had the experience; otherwise it would be a struggling affair. Money would be the vital juice for business and like most entrepreneurs, you would not have sufficient of it to maintain your company for long. Fortunately, you can run an Internet company with very little money, as compared to a conventional one. There are many successful one-man run Internet companies, and depending on the nature of your business, you can certainly start by doing everything yourself. I did all the things myself and in the process become some sort of expert in it. You can also do it.

As a first time entrepreneur, your greatest concern would be your operating cost and if you can control it well, you will win part of the battle. Entrepreneurs normally will rely on their life savings to kick start their ventures, or they could rope in some partners. If they have property assets, they should also consider charging it for loans to finance their endeavors. Although it is a bit risky, it does give the entrepreneur a sense of mission, in this case, an important one, where there is no room for failure: sort of burning the bridge after crossing it.

Your Conception

"What can I sell online?" is the most asked question when Internet Marketing is the topic of discussion. Most people would love to be their own boss and be able to push their own brand product using the net. Unfortunately, the reality is that only a small number of people will manage to do so as viable ideas are a very scarce commodity. However, it is not an impossible thing as you will be able to find many of them on the net. There are also many types of services and software programs available on the net, and you might get that spark of an idea if you were willing to do your research there. Although you will come across many ideas, they are actually derived from some other existing ideas. You will need that creative streak to juggle the ideas around, and on a good day, your new idea might just sprout out from no where. Idea creation is an art and when your idea gets flowing, many more ideas will follow. The problem is to get your first idea. If you were to look back many years past, you might just remember that you use to have many ideas before. Dig it up, revive it and give it a new twist. You might then be on the way to a new Internet Marketing journey! If after all attempts, you still fail to come up with any viable idea, then the only recourse is to sell someone else's product. Sometimes, you can combine other people's product and make it into a new item, so go and take a second look at products that are available out there and juggle them around. Take a look at small local producers that have not embraced the internet. Use theirs.

Think global and you might just have a new marketing idea and for all you know, it might just be lying in your back yards all this while!

Ideas usually start from a question or a problem. If you are scratching your head as to what new thing to think of, try asking yourself questions like 'what if I were to add this thing to that' or 'can I put in three wheels instead of the usual four' sorts of query. Or pose the questions to your children instead? You will be surprised by their answers! With a small insignificant idea for a start, you can add some other ideas to it and make it bigger. The thing is ideas evolve and if you play around with it, it becomes viable. I would like to advise you to come up with an idea that is unique. When it is unique, people who come across it will open their eyes and gawk at it. In Internet Marketing, stale products don't get a second look. You should make it as weir as possibly can, so that people will pass it around to their friends. Whether they buy it or not is another matter, as long as they create that viral buzz for you.

When you have that idea, what to do next?

You would do well to identify who and where are your competitors. Try to make your product as unique as you possibly can so that you will have less direct competition. Some people think that when they take the path of Internet Marketing, they will give their product a boost, but in reality, it is more like going out there and competing with all the other guys. The internet is a global market place and not a small local affair, and you have to be dressed up in your best suit! Better still; dress up in full battle gear! You will need to think and rethink about your product. Give yourself sufficient time to explore other possibilities. Please do not be mislead by those scam artist out there that use to promise people that a few million bucks are for their taking in a matter of a few weeks of work!

How to make it

When you have nailed down your product, the next step is to see how you can manufacture it. Intangible items like software and info books will not pose a problem, but tangible items will need all your ingenuity. Assuming that you have created a tangible product and your prototype has been rigorously tested, your next step is to see whether you can manufacture it. When you bring your idea to someone else, you have to be careful so that it is not stolen from you. If possible, make the other party sign a non disclosure clause before you discuss the product.

If you have enough resources, then by all means make that product yourself. But like most newcomers where there is neither experience nor abundance of capital, your best recourse is to outsource it to a contract manufacturer. Where Internet Marketing is concerned, there are many new things to learn, so it would be advisable to concentrate on the marketing aspect and leave the manufacturing to a third party. Even with the manufacturing being outsourced, there are other areas to take care of like the logistics, fulfillments, warehousing and managing. As far as outsourcing is concerned, whether locally or in third countries, there is the question of maintaining a consistent quality level throughout. There is the danger of disruption in production, which can adversely impact your company's image, so you also have to thread with caution. If possible, sell a product that is simple to make as the number of problems will be reduced to a minimum level.

Other matters

Before you can proceed with the manufacturing, there are issues like product protection. You will have to determine whether you need to file for patents and trade marks. Depending on which country you are operating from, there are different needs as regard to filing for patents. As patent filings are expensive and time consuming, you should research on the issue thoroughly. In certain circumstances, protecting your trade secrets instead is more viable. Product protection is an essential part of managing your assets and you should take sometime to read up on it. Doing it wrong will cost you dearly, but not protecting your assets is fool-hardy. Intellectual property protections should be done in the earliest, and not as an after thought.

Chapter 3

Marketing Proper

Website

In order to put your message to the rest of the world, you will use a web site. No, not just any web site, but a well optimized (functions well) website! Too often, people think that after they have designed their web site and make it live, they can forget about it. It is true if only they would like to remain invisible to the rest of the world! Would you like to become invisible and attract no visitors? Certainly not!

Also, some people believed that their website should be their showpiece, so they go all the way to design it to look like as if they were going to attend the Oscar Award Night. But if yours is the window to your Internet Marketing exercise, there are certain rules that you have to follow in order to get 'traffic' to your business. Yes, Internet Marketing is all about getting as many people to visit your web site as far as possible. It is also called 'traffic'. A business website is quite different from a personal website. You have to 'optimized' it so that the 'search engines' can identify what you do and how to 'rank' you in their display of search results (called SERP). For the uninitiated, the search engines rely on 'keywords' to categorized what they find on the websites. And they wholly rely on 'text' to do each categorization. What it means is that if your website contains only graphics and no text, the search engines (those that uses robot programs) will not be able to identify what is the message all about and thus will not categorize it. When that happens, your website will not be found by people who type queries unto the search engines when they do a search (80% of people use search engines to search for information). You are for all intent, invisible on the net. Surprisingly, not many people (especially the senior ones) know that the internet works on such principals. They though it worked like the good old telephone directory, where when you registered for your telephone, you are automatically listed and so can be found under the alphabetical format! Part of the reason is because the internet was not designed for people searching for information, but it was designed to connect different data (US military) servers, each with a coded identity. Search was an after thought, and search engines like Yahoo and Alter Vista only came into existence later when people were finding it difficult to locate each other on the internet.

What is the significance of 'keyword' to your internet marketing then? Everything! Yes, from the name of your website to the wordings of your web messages and every other thing that you have not thought of yet. Even graphics and pictures have to be coded with keyword, and so are audio and videos as well. Otherwise, they cannot be categorized and get found. Of course when we say you cannot be found, we are referring to those search listings that are called 'natural listings' thrown out by search engines. You can be found if you were to 'pay for inclusion' in the search results, or you subscribe to 'pay-per-click' advertisements with the search engines. These paid for listings are listed on the left hand corner of Google and are distinguishable from the natural listing on the right hand column. It is however not distinguishable in both Yahoo and MSN and whether it is considered ethical or not, I will leave you to decide. These methods are also expensive and no sane entrepreneur (those who are on a tight budget) can afford to rely on such methods on a continuous basis. You should try to put your website listing using the natural searches as far as possible, failing which, you should then only consider PPC (paid) insertions.

Website name

What is in a name, you might ask? Well, for Internet Marketing, if you choose your website name like you choose your children's name, then you could be making a big mistake. Sometime back, when we have search directories (different from search engines) like Yahoo, it was wise to choose names which begin with the letter 'a'. At that time, the listings were listed according to the English alphabetical order, so if your website name starts with the alphabet 'a', then it will be listed at the front row in each category. But now, most search listings don't list in that manner, and instead list on their keywords. Thus, if your website name includes the keyword then the search engines would rank it high when that keyword is searched. And it would not be in alphabetical order either, only in the order of importance according to each search engine's 'algorithm'.

A search engine algorithm is a proprietary computer program that takes certain values (a few hundred determinants) into consideration in order to rank each website. Algorithms are secret formulas and search engines don't reveal them to the public. They also change it regularly, sometimes daily, much to the exasperation of 'search engine optimizers' (SEO in short) whose job is to tweak websites to rank high on the search engine listings. At the present time, it would be wise to name your website with at least a keyword, where keyword would describe the kind of activity that your site would like to project. For example; if your web activity includes selling flowers, you can choose a name like www.freshFlowersDaily.com or www.143FlowerPetals.com or some other combinations. As search engines change their algorithms constantly, whether they will continue to give value to website name with keyword infused is uncertain, so webmasters must continually update themselves.

Now, having chosen an appropriate name may not be all there is to it. You have to pray that it is available for registration. You will have to register it with the domain registrar. Then again, you will have to choose what domain to register it under. Here your first choice should be .com rather then .net as people normally will search for sites ending with dotcom first. However, as there are only a limited number of dotcoms available, it might be better to buy it from previous owners, provided it comes with a reasonable price. Registered domain names are like real world properties and its purchase is transacted through a willing buyer willing seller basis. You might feel that the asking price might be expensive, but if you were to look at it from another angle, you can also sell it off later and make a profit. Just imagine, people are comfortable with buying expensive cars which depreciates the moment they drive it out of the showroom but they cringed noisily when they buy their domain name which in most likelihood appreciates in value later on! Domain names should be treated like antiques, especially the .com types!

If you already have an enterprise name, choosing a web name for your website might be more difficult. Using the same name might not be available, but since your main focus is on the internet, prioritizing the web name in your branding exercise should take precedence.

PROMOTIONS

Banner Ads & pay for inclusion
An internet marketing business must be prepared to advertise its presence. On the net itself, there are the basic banner ads that you can see in most commercial websites. Then there are other ad-sponsored activities plus the ever popular pay-per-click advertisements with the search engines. On a more sophisticated platform, you have the Google Adsense where it is based on contextual contents on other people's website. Indeed, if you were to take a closer look, the internet seems to be powered wholly by advertising dollars. This is not surprising because as more and more enterprises enter the online field, there is a real need to attract buyers to their websites. One easy and immediate way is to pay for adverts, either with search engines or with popular websites that already have plenty of traffic. For anyone new to the net, there is no better way than to put up the adverts and get immediate 'eyeballs' to their website. Compared to real world advertising campaigns, the online exercise cost much less, plus there is a possibility of tracking the response in real time. Thus return on investment (ROI)

on advert spending can be evaluated with a degree of certainty.

PPC

Pay-per-click (PPC) is the pay for inclusion listings introduced by search engines like Overture and Google as an easy way to draw traffic to websites. It is based on keywords and advertisers can choose which keyword they would like their websites to be listed. With Google, their pay per click will be listed on the right hand corner. Yahoo, which also owns Overture, will have the pay per click listings mingled among the natural listings and advertisers can have a high listing if they are willing to pay for it. When surfers click on the website links in the search listings, the advertisers will be charged an agreed amount, ranging from ten cents to ten over dollars each. Whether the prospect (surfer) buys or not, the advertisers will have to pay. Using this method, new websites (which will normally not be listed in the search listings) can attract prospects to their website since they can now be listed on the first few pages of the SERP (surfers don't normally go beyond the first three pages of the listings).

The cost of PPC depends on the keywords selected, with popular terms like 'realty' and 'casino' going for ten dollars a click to less popular terms like 'cabinet selves' costing ten cents. PPC schemes are very popular with advertisers because it is a fast way to attract prospects. It is also highly controllable in the sense that you can decide when and where to advertise. You can even stop it at midnight and resume the next morning, all within a click of the mouse from your desktop or a button on your cell phone, anywhere in the world! The other good point is that you can get immediate response from your campaign. You will know where they click from and whether your ad copy is effective or not. For local searches, you can also incorporate your phone number so that when they click on your PPC link, they are taken straight to your telephone.

Since the dotcom bubble burst in 2001, many new enterprises have been using PPC programs to attract customers. They are people who rely solely on PPC to survive and some of them even become experts in it. Many have succeeded, but there were also failures, so you have to learn how to use it justifiably. Search engines are electrified by the PPC programs as they find that a large portion of their revenues (some as much as 65%) is derived from it. There are also entrepreneurs who live wholly on PPC schemes to make a living. One of the least known attributes of running a PPC campaign is that you will sharpen your copy writing skills, especially if you use Google Adwords. This is because they allow you to tweak those twenty words that you are allowed on your advertisements whenever you choose. In fact, if you start off with an advert that can't seem to attract people to click on, your advert will go down a few levels and you will be asked to rewrite your advert slogan or they pull you off the campaign! How is that for ROI? This doesn't happen with off-line conventional advertisements. However, like all advertising campaigns, you learn by practice. There are also some unsavory matters with PPC campaigns, like 'click fraud' (unknown syndicate's gang up to click on your advert and gets to share part of your payments) and spammers (who is more interested to get your email address than anything else), which might deter some from using it. Eventually, PPC schemes might morph into a more mature scheme whereby you only pay when someone clicks on your link and buy from you. No buy means no pay. That might happen sooner than later if the click fraud issue gets out of hand, and when advertisers shy away from using the program.

PRESS RELEASES

On-line press releases for new enterprises are a must because it is easy and cost effective, as compared to the conventional off-line printed type. Everything can be activated from the desktop and there is no need to shuttle the copy writing to and fro with the publishing media. Your press release can also be much targeted and you can direct to the person that matters most. Not only that, most off-line Medias will also tap unto these online news feeds and republish them in their newspapers and magazines.

The electronic medium has afforded any news worthy press releases to travel wide and far, sometimes almost within the same day. No wonder the local papers are feeling the pinch from ever shrinking advertising dollars. The situation could get worse when more people are finding out about the effectiveness of on-line press releases. Just imagine your very local centric news being broadcasted half a world away and getting unexpected positive response from there instead of your expected but underperformed response from your local townsfolk! This is the 'new media' they are talking about, so get a piece of the action. You can be sure that your local Medias don't want you to know about, least they have to answer to their shareholders about their shrinking revenues!

Conventional Medias

Like all new enterprises, a dose of start up conventional off-line advertising campaign can bring in fast awareness from the public. Although yours is an internet company, a little bit of advertising in the local paper cannot be bad. If you can get the local TV station to give you a mention, it would be much better. This is especially so if your product is a unique one and has a global potential. Local town folks will be proud if one of their own countrymen has a solution to a world problem! Still, conventional advertising is more expensive than the online version, so you have to allot your budget appropriately. If you are doing a launching, you can perhaps do a local promotion just to test market first before you go global. This way, little mistakes can be rectified before it becomes out of your control. When your local promotion works, you will have more confidence to move to a bigger market.

TRAFFIC CREATION
Listing with Directories
When you put up a website, you are also putting up a message. You want an audience for your message. However, if you do not announce your presence in the media, either through electronic or conventional channels, no body will know you existed. Even the search engines with all their computer robotics might, might not stump unto you. So if nothing else is done, you will remain invisible. This is for real, and too many people, who have not read enough, will unfortunately be ignorant of this fact. To them, if they built the website, people will automatically come to visit.

About 95% of these websites out there has got no visitors. Even those that are put up by established companies faced the same fate. But then again, their CEO's are too busy with other things and could not be bothered. Some don't even know about it. Some are even worse, as they had reluctantly put up their website just because their neighbors or their competitors had one. If you are depending on the net to conduct your business, then you have no choice but to make it your top priority to make your website very visible to the search engines as well as your prospective clients. It is a new ball game (more so for those from the less developed countries) and there is too much to learn. Internet Marketing is all about traffic and if nobody knows about you, you will have no visitors and also no sales.

Luckily, there are ways to make your web searchable, and they fall into two categories, one of which is called on-site optimization (a term meaning to tweak your website) and the other is called off-site optimization (something you do outside your website). You can learn more about these optimization methods from web consultants but I will give you the basics here. Optimization methods are dependant on the search engine's algorithms, and since it changes quite often, techniques have to be updated often as well, but once you know the basics, updating your knowledge will be easy. If you find it a hassle, you can always pay someone to do the job, but I would advise that you at least know some basics first; otherwise you could be taken for a ride by scammers and fraudsters.

On-site optimization
This is about tweaking the web pages so that when a search engine robot (computer programs coded to read the HTML

of your web page) comes snooping (yes, they come crawling), they will be given appropriate information about what message the web page is all about. After visiting the website, the robots will report back to the search engine and a cache copy is kept at the search engine's data server. The search engines will then interpret and rank (over a hundred determinants) of the page according to its relevancy to the selected keyword. Listing will then be sorted out on its SERP with the most relevant page on top, followed by pages which are less relevant. It performs this task using its proprietary algorithms, which takes into consideration hundreds of variables including the number of website linking inwards, keyword saturations, among others.

On-page tweaking will mean that your HTML will show your page title, keywords at the beginning of the page, followed by keywords spattered over the page in a natural pattern, and also Meta tags. Since the search engines are known (by inference) to take into consideration hundreds of variables in order to place a ranking (in respect to other web pages) on the page, it would be beyond the scope of this book to mention all of it here. You can however learn more of these various factors by visiting Search Engine Optimization (SEO) forum sites, but it will take years in order to master it. If you can't afford the time, then pay someone to do it. Another way is to go to websites with top listings and open its 'source code' and research on it. Search engine robots can only read text codes on your web page, it does not read java scripts, image diagrams, and flash animations so if your page is designed with little text and plenty of animations and graphics, then the page will get a very low ranking. So you will have to balance whether you put up a text heavy page that don't wow visitors but ranks well or a page with lots of animation that wows your visitor but ranks poorly on the SERP. When your business depends heavily on site traffic, you would be advisable to put up a text heavy page so that it will have a better ranking such that it can be found from the natural search listings.

But how much text you might ask? Just take a look at Blogs and you will get an idea. You will find that many blog web sites are getting very high rankings, especially with search engines like Google. And they not only have plenty of text, but also constant updates as Google treat it as an active website and so relevant to what a surfer wants. I however do not agree to such an interpretation, but that is nothing, the important thing is that you have to design your webpage to present it well to the search engines first. The alternative is to pay for inclusion.

Sometimes a graphic paints better than a thousand words, so if you need one on your page, put alternate tags (an accompany text description of the image file) to tell the search engine what your image is all about. Since there is also an image and video (reads You Tube) search with the major search engines, tagging your image file with alternate text is a must as your image can be easily found, even though your web page might not show up in the first few pages of the SERP. Regarding flash opening pages, they normally rank poorly, and although Google robots does detect them now, it will take some time before webmaster can embed effectively the keyword in the file for the benefit of the search robots.

Page title

The title of the site will be the first thing the search engine robots go for in determining what the theme of the webpage is about. You must put in the HTML title (which is not visible unless you open up the source code tag) appropriately, otherwise the search engine will place your listing in the wrong category, or if it cannot determine the theme of your page, it might not list it at all. Unfortunately, not many webmaster know about this basic requirement and you will find many websites that has no title (to the search engines) at all! Titles should also be descriptive enough to tell what the theme is, in not too many words. What should you write in the title if you have come up with an entire new item? Supposing that your title is a description of a new product, like 'ZZAXX', the search engine will place your page at the top (could be the only one) of the listing in a category that is 'ZZAXX'. Although you are now in the number one listing, nobody will key in this keyword unless of course you are also letting people know what this new 'ZZAXX' thing is all about in the conventional Medias like TV, newspaper and other off-line Medias. When you are describing something that is entirely new, then try to include a word or two that is of common knowledge, so that the search engine can at least list you in a category that people knows of. What is in a name, you might ask? But in the cyber world, name is everything and everything is keyword! Do your researches before you come up with your page title, especially when you are dealing with a new product.

Let us now go deeper into this title tag.

In the HTML code of a web site, TITLE tags look like this one (let us take a cake shop for an example):

<TITLE>Dallas Cakes – taste like home bake, made to your order</Title>

To view the HTML code of any site, choose 'View, Source' from your browser toolbar or right click anywhere on the page and choose 'view source code'.

When it comes to titles, you will have to research your combination of effective keywords such that it will describe in the shortest words what your website is all about. In the example above, I have included the place name Dallas so that if there is a listing of cake shops in the Dallas area, this website will stand a chance of being listed in the SERP. Noticed that I have included the words like 'home bake' and 'made to order', so if there are surfers who key in those words (which are related cake terms from a search perspective), this website would likely be found. This title will also tell the search engines more about the site, as compared to a title like 'Dallas Cakes'.

Meta description tags.

Next in importance are the Meta description tags. It is found in the HTML code just after the title tags. The META Keywords Tag is still worth including within a site's HTML code, because it helps in telling to the search engines about the page contents. However, not all search engines take this Meta description tag into consideration due mainly to

- 41 -

spammers using this entry point to mislead the search engines.

Here is what the Meta description tag looks like:-

<META name="keywords" content="cakes ,home bake, make to order, Dallas, deliver to home, fresh, arrangements, seasonal cakes">

As Meta tags were used to spam the search engines, it is advisable not to stuff it with too many key phrases. Short and sharp is the best policy.

Meta description is the HTML description of your page content and is not visible unless you click the 'view' dropdown from the file button of your Internet Explorer. In Mozilla Firefox, click on the view button at the top, and then drill down to the source code tag to see the HTML code. Although not normally visible from your webpage, it is the text that the search engines used to describe your SERP listings (the twenty odd letters that the search engines describe your website). If you have beautiful Meta descriptions (good copy writing), people might just click on your SERP links even though it is at the bottom of the listings. On the other hand, if your Meta description doesn't excite the surfer, it might not even be clicked even though it sits at the top position!

Now, not many people know the existence of the Meta description tag, and even less people know how to make full use of it. Just open some pages you find on the net and open up its source code and you should not be surprised to find no Meta tags at all. But how do the search engines display those short twenty words if your site does not have the Meta description? Well, they will then probably grab the first few sentences of your text and display them in the SERP, hoping that it will best describe your site. But it might not pull visitors, so it is best that you tell the search engines what to describe your website, and that is through proper and intelligent copy writing on your Meta description. This is the only place where you have a chance to tell the search engine what to describe your site. However, search engines don't always take your Meta description into consideration for they may use the one from D'MOZ which you had register (they don't accept any more indexing now) before. If you find that your website description from D'MOZ shown on the SERP is not appropriate enough to pull in the visitors, and you want it changed, then all you have to do is to insert the 'NOODP' tag in your Meta description tag and the search engines will use your own Meta tag description in the SERP. In short, you can control those short twenty or something words that the search engines placed in their SERP. Your copy writing skills here will be tested to the fullest. Of course the other thing that you have to do is to check your log files and monitor what keyword phrases will pull in the visitors most. Not many people do it either!

Title/subtitle (the visible part)

If your title needs many words, it is better to break it down with a subtitle. In webpage terminology, there are various paragraphs like H1 and H2 where the former is accorded more importance than the later. You will have to put your main title in H1 and your subtitle in H2. This will tell the search engine which is your main theme and which is your lesser theme. Next to the HTML title, H1 and H2 are next in importance, so put your text appropriately at the visible top of your web page. If you have an image file at the top, make sure to include the alternate text so that the search engine knows what is in the image file as they can't read its content. Another consideration that is of importance is to give individual titles to different pages. The reason is that you will most probably have a different topic for different pages and if you differentiate your titles, the search engines will have an easier job of ranking your page according to its various categories. If the search engines can't read what your page is about, it will just ignore it and you will loose by not being ranked. Your HTML title code for the different pages should also reflect on what you put in those pages.

Keyword density

Keyword stuffing is the technique of putting plenty of keywords all over the page. It was used to get top billing for the particular keyword, but the search engines has got wise to this method by webmasters to hook winking them. It is now advisable to include no more than two percent of the total text with keywords and with search technologies improving, webmaster should write their text in a natural fashion as far as possible. This is the result of improving 'contextual' technology used by the search engines where 'artificial intelligence' is used to interpret search queries and a premium is put on natural language sentences. In the near future, we should be able to key in a whole query sentence and get relevant answers at the first click.

Navigation

If you have a webpage that is crammed with lots of things, including advertisements, flashing images and what not, try to view it from the search engine robots point of view to see whether it is confusing or not. If the search engines find it difficult to navigate, it might not want to rank the page at all. As some webmasters are ignorant of search engine workings, they could be carried away in their designs so much so that the page becomes difficult to navigate, not only to humans, but to the robots as well. What the search engines see is quite different from what the human eyes see. In internet marketing, you have to design your website to be search engine friendly as well as to be human being friendly. Do them a favor on both counts and don't frustrate them, or they will leave in haste. Not many people, including your web designer know how the search engine views your web page, and because of this ignorance, many web sites are invisible and cannot be found in the SERP.

Internal links

Internal links are the links that connects your different pages and it is important to give them appropriate descriptions like 'find out more about our returns policy' instead of just showing 'click here'. You have also got to make sure that the links are not broken or worse still, leads to an error '403' destination. It is bad design and search robots don't take kindly to such carelessness. When you put a link to another web site, it is often difficult to know when that link has changed, so as part of your maintaining work, try checking every link on your site at least once a month, or you can use a link checker program. You have to be especially careful as some links can lead the robots to a continuous loop and this type of trap is a no go area. Out-bound links should also be constantly checked just so that you are showing others that your links are not dead ends. A little extra effort goes a long way to get good SERP rankings and also to give the search robots a good reason to come more often to do their updating. When robots don't come, it is reason to be anxious, as there is such a thing as search engines 'banning' websites. If your website is being banned, you will have to write in to them to appeal, and because they are so busy, you might not get your request answered.

Robot text file

Most knowledgeable webmasters have a 'robots text' file in their websites. A robots text file purpose is to give instructions to robots as to what they can do like which pages they can index, as well as the time they are allowed. Of course search engines don't have to obey such commands, but generally all the major search engines (that matters) do obey them. If you have a website that contains a lot of pages, you might prefer that some of the pages not to be indexed just to reduce the bandwidth (more bandwidth usage means more maintaining cost) when they come visiting. You can tell them what pages can be read and what pages are out of bounds. Sometimes, certain of your web pages might have a time sensitive content which you would not prefer the search engine to index, so putting an appropriate command in the robot text file when to leave it alone might cut your bandwidth usage. When you have no robot text files, then the search engines will assume doing things as they deem fit. Web sites which are popular also attract all types of robots and many of them are a nuisance. Putting a command to allow only the three major search engines to crawl your site will become good web site management practice.

Site maps

Site maps are a diagrammatic means to show visitors what to find at a glance. It is especially useful when the site contains huge number of pages where navigating among them is a problem. Although it is designed for human use, it has also become a useful tool for search robots as having one is an indication that the site is friendly and navigable. You will get a better ranking when you have a site map.

Alternate tags for image files

As search engine robots have difficulty in interpreting image files like jpeg, gif and flash, you should help them by inserting alternate text so that the search engines can categorize them correctly. The major search listings have a section on image searches, so it would be useful if your images can be found there as well. There is a trend now for surfers to search from the images section, perhaps because it is a faster way to find things, especially if it better rendered in an image form. Image files get ranking as well, but it is not very clear how the search engines rank them, or whether humans are employed to do it. I found that if the webpage containing it ranks high, then the image file also have high rankings in the image SERP. If you are dealing with a product that is better off being shown in an image form, then you should make sure it is optimized to rank high in the image SERP. Presently, there is no PPC for images search, but it might be introduced in the future, as many people find it easier to nail down the relevant webpage through the image SERP section.

Viewing too much text is getting a lot of eye strains and elderly people will find it more efficient to view them instead of the mountain of texts. Likewise for animated files like flash, most of the search engines give it a miss, but with further advances in technology, the day will come when they can also be recognized by the robots. Images, animations and video files might be the next wave of searches, so getting prepared for it would be a good move. If what you see in You Tube is any indication of mass adoption, then there is no doubt that search methodologies will change to gear towards such demand.

On another angle, as more and more people are accessing the net through their cell phones, web pages will have to cater to these users as well. Mobile Internet Marketing might be quite different in that there might be shorter text files to cater to the smaller mobile screens. Mobile SERPs are culled from mobile web sites, so you do need a separate page for these searches.

Server location

It used to be a one set of SERP no matter where you do your searching, but it is now the normal trend that different SERP will appear for different locations (country wise). If you are searching in the US, your SERP will be different from the one if you are in the UK or Asia. The search engines like Google, MSN and Yahoo will recognize your location and will serve you results that they think will better reflect the relevancy of the web sites. For example, if you enquire about a cake shop in the Vancouver area, you will get SERP that have many websites with a Vancouver address. Even if you do not key in any area name, the search engines can still identify where you are located by your server address, and in most probability, will serve you listings that are appropriate to your area. Of course the search engines will first have to identify the physical address of the web sites concerned, otherwise, it will not be able to use location based algorithms. What this means to the webmaster is that if your target market is within a small geographical region, you will be better of putting your server near such a region, but if your target market encompasses a wider region, you will have to incorporate regional web addresses and have servers there as well. For example, if your market includes the UK besides the US markets, you will be better off having a dotUS and a dotUK address as the search engines give some priority to include local companies in their SERP. It might all add up to additional running cost though.

Browser compatibility

As there are four major browsers, what looks good on one might not be so for the others. Since Internet Explorer commands at least seventy five percent of users, it would be logical to design your webpage to look good in it. You also need to test in on Mozilla Firefox, Mac, and Opera browsers to see how the page is been handled. Obviously your webpage will look different in these browsers, but if there are no major issues, then slight differences can still be tolerated.

As more and more users are turning to their mobile devices to go on the web, it would be advisable to have another mobile version of your webpage. You can design your main web site to redirect visitors to your mobile page once a mobile surfer is detected. Mobile browsers work differently from their desk top counterparts, so having your web site tested with the major browsers like window mobile, symbiam, opera mobile and linux is important.

Quality contents

Search engines love page contents, the more the better. It will give you good marks if you update your contents frequently, just like Blogs. When we talk about content, it must be on the same theme as the title, so if your title is 'Blue Roses', your content must be based on blue roses and anything else related to it. If your content does not rhyme with your title, then the search engines will not consider it relevant, and will ignore your page. When your content is updated constantly, the search engines will consider it favorably and hike up your rank. The top positions in the SERP are normally considered the most relevant pages for their particular keyword category. They are also being considered as 'authority' site, so attaining it should be the goal of every webmaster.

Quick downloading

People loved to cram their websites with all sorts of text, graphics and animations because it makes it look cool. However, they don't realize that surfers out there are normally impatient people, and they will just click away when crammed web pages take a long time to download. So you will have to balance between a webpage that looks good, but slow to download and a page that don't look so cool, but fast to render. Generally, text heavy pages get rendered much faster than those with large graphics, and telling your web designers what is required before hand will get you a good functional website instead of one that is slow to download. If you are not aware as to where your page download speed is compared to others, try Google SERP or Mozilla homepages and you will see where your web site stand.

Keyword proximity

There was a time when webmasters stuffed their web page with an overdose of keywords such that the text copy of the page looks artificial and unnatural. Their intention was to fool the search engines to get high relevant rankings in the SERP. However, the search engines got wise to such tactics, and it will not only look negatively at such a technique, but it will also give negative grade for keywords that are close to each other. They called it spamming, and consider such unnatural copy undeserved of any ranking. The right thing to do now is first write your copy with the search engines in mind, then go through it, read it loud if possible and edit it to make your copy natural. The number of keywords, or better known in search engine terminology as 'keyword density' should be less than two percent of the total. As search engines rely more on 'contextual' interpretations of your page, you should not spattered your page text with the singular and plural versions of your keywords. If it is difficult to read, then you have to edit it to read as natural as possible. Another method is to intersperse your keywords with the noun, adjective or verb versions so you can cover all your bases. Remember, your copy has to look and sound natural all the time, otherwise you will be considered a spammer.

Website log statistics

A good practice of Internet Marketing is to allot some time to monitor website traffic and to analyze who are your visitors. Most web hosting packages do include statistics and log files so that you can be informed as to the number of visitors. As these are very basic systems, it would be advisable to subscribe to other more advance programs that will be able to trace what your visitors do when they come to visit. One of the benefits of Internet Marketing is that you can analyze how your visitors behave, what they are attracted to, and what sells. There are also system analysts that can help your marketing campaign by analyzing what works and what is not working by studying your website traffic. You can also use the free Google Analytics program to see what keywords your visitors use to find your web site. If possible, use an advance web site analytics program that can tell you who comes and for how long on every of your page. It does cost more, but then it will give you a better picture of your visitor's profile.

Off-site optimization

SEO

Search Engine Optimization (SEO) is an essential element used in fine tuning your website to make it searchable and increase traffic. If you are in business, you need visitors and plenty of it. You can either pay for it through banner ads placed in other people's website, or PPC with search engines or tweaking it yourself for very little money. I will now tell you the methods used by SEO consultants and the other SEO fraternities. However, SEO techniques are not definitive concepts, but they are mostly culled from the experiences of webmasters. Search engines don't normally tell how they rank websites, but on and off, they do reveal some of their views, especially towards techniques by webmasters that they consider unsavory. In cases where they consider as tricks to hoodwink search engines, they might ban the website concerned. SEO is slotted into two categories called 'white hat' and 'black hat'. White hat techniques are approved by search engines while black hat ones are not. I will tell you about the white hat ones. You can learn more about black hat techniques on other web sites. Before that, let us look at how search engines rank websites.

How do search engines rank websites?

Search engines normally take into considerations hundreds of variable in order to give ranking to web pages. They use their own propriety programs called algorithms to rank each web page. They also don't tell what these determinants are. Here are some of the important known ones.

Links

Links (from outside), and plenty of it, is the main determinant to get high ranking in the SERP. When you have links from other sites, it is considered as a form of endorsement for your web page. The more links, the more endorsement and if yours has the most endorsements, it will be regarded as the authority site for that particular keyword. Why would others link to your site then? You need to have something good or something relevant before others will give a link pointing to your website.

As an example, suppose you are the creator of a computer program that perform certain functions, and you are allowing others to download (could be free or paying) the program from your site. And supposing that this other website has a content that is referring to the program that you have created, the other website will put a link pointing to your site as they want their visitors to try the program. Now, putting a link is not enough as the accompanying 'anchor text' which briefly describes your content is equally important, otherwise the link is not considered to be that valuable. Anchor text is the short text that briefly describes the main feature of your web site in the hypertext link pointing (clickable) to your web address.

The reason why links are so important is that the whole World Wide Web (WWW) is consisting of links from one to the others. Without the links, it becomes a hassle navigating around. When you have a lot of one-way inbound (all pointing to you without you pointing back) links, you are considered as being popular. Yes, popularity also works on the internet. And popularity means money.

As far as SEO is concerned, creating links (one-way links) is the fastest way to rank high in the SERP. It is so important that some people are willing to pay for one-way links from others. Yes, you can buy your way to the top! But search engines look at it negatively, as it is tantamount to cheating, and they have banned some sites that were believed to have bought their links from others. Search engines will put your site on the suspect list if they find that you managed to get plenty of one-way links all of a sudden, or all in a short span of time. They equate this to link buying or even worst, linking you to participating in illegal (to the search engines) 'link farms'.

At one time, exchanging links (also known as reciprocal links) with others was the fastest way to build up your links, but it is not popular now as people suspects that search engines has begun playing down its value. Another new method of trying to hoodwink the search engines is to use a 'three way link'. It works like this. Say, you have three different sites, called A, B and C. Now, all you have to do is from A, put a link to B. From B, put a link to C, and from C, put a link back to A. Each site will now have a 'one-way link' from one to the others. To a search engine, it does not see a two way reciprocal link, so it will think that it is a genuine one-way link endorsement. But search engines will get smart to this ruse in due time, so it is advisable that you don't get your one-way links using this method.

Syndicate your content

Since search engines give higher ranks for sites that have plenty of contents, one way to achieve good ranking is to publish articles and put it either on your website, or let others publish it with the proviso your article has a one-way link back to your own site. Contents is still king when it comes to achieving high rankings, and contents that are regularly upgraded will even be better. You can write articles, newsletters or short essays on topics that you are good at and allow 'articles directories' to publish them. The good thing about others publishing your content is that you can put a 'link back' from the 'resource box' of your content. You are also free to put in an appropriate anchor text that describes what your site is about. Now, writing articles allows you to stamp your 'brand' on the net. These articles published in high traffic sites are often read by many people, and when your articles (many, not just two or three) are well read, your 'brand' will somehow stick in their minds. It is also a great form of free advertisement for you. However, please do not write useless articles that seem like a rehash of what others have written, because it will reflect badly on you. Before writing anything, do a proper research on the net to see what is already published out there or you might be not regarded at all. Remember, when you put up anything out on the net, you must stamp an aura of authority, and in case you are not yet there, do more reading before you start writing your masterpiece. If writing is not your fort, you can pay a 'ghost writer' to write for you. People read articles on the net to learn and find out more and it seems to be the main use of the internet. They want to learn from authorities and experts, so do not write about 'teaching others how to write an e-book' when you yourself have not even written one! There are a lot of pretenders out there on the net, but keeping up on pretending is a costly futile occupation.

Directories

There was a time when every SEO exercise starts with going to search directories to get one-way links. At that time, registration of websites with the directories was mostly free. It was also then the early days of Google, and which not many people know about. There were then hundreds of free sites to get your links, but things have changed now, with many of them turning themselves into pay for inclusion directories for survival. Few of them are left now, so getting that free link is no more a viable move. Just in case you are attracted to those who offer to submit your sites to hundreds of directories for a fee, do not fall into the trap as these are not directories, but just some unranked websites that was bought up for the purpose of acting as search directories!

Then there are others that will give you a link, provided you also put up a reciprocal link in return. However, major search engines like Google, Yahoo and MSN do not give any ranking for these so called directories as they consider them 'link farms' and thus a negative connotation. But in case you still want to be linked from such websites, you should find out to see what their Google page rank is first. To see the Google page rank on a page, you must install the Google toolbar and have the 'page rank' enabled. Some of them are actually banned sites and have no page ranks at all. So beware! It might be better to pay for inclusion in Yahoo's directory and if your site is accepted (they have an out of this world no guarantee inclusion clause even if you pay them 299 dollars!), the link is a high value link. Links from websites that are in the same theme or business are treated favorably by the major search engines as they treat it as a strong endorsement. So write to these high ranking websites to cajole them to give you a link. You should offer something in return of course, like writing an article linking to them or some other offers.

Blogs

Blogs are a kind of online journal, and because it has contents that are frequently updated, the search engines liked them so much that it accords them high rankings. It is not uncommon to find Blogs being found in the first twenty results of SERP. Blogs can take up much of your time, but if you put up one and link it to your business web site, it will help in improving the ranking of your main site. Further more, bloggers, when they are alerted to your blog, will probably pop over to take a look at what you have in your blog, and in so doing, might also click on the link to your website. There is a kind of camaraderie there among bloggers that you don't see in other places. They will also place links to your web site. However, as Blogs gets into the main stream, crowding becomes inevitable, so putting up good contents and getting people to come over to read will be more difficult. Your Blog also need traffic. Moreover, there are other variants like audio and video Blogs that are edging for people's attention, so you need to be creative to be counted. As it is early days for audio and video Blogs, expect it to get mainstream later, embedding audio and video files in your web site might be the next best thing to do.

Forums

You will be able to find forum sites on almost any topic and participating (by commenting) in them can lead to more traffic to your site. When you put up comments at forum sites, you will normally be allowed to also include a link to your website, so you have another inbound from the forum site. However, as there are a lot of outbound links from the forum site, its value is diluted, and search engines do not give it high values. But because you get a link, curious surfers might still click on it to take a closer look at your site. Forum sites (and Blogs as well) also might put a tag called the 'no follow' code which is intended to tell the search engines to not crawl the link. The reason is that if your site has a lot of out going links, then you are 'bleeding' yourself from gaining 'page rank' (a Google rating, from 1 to 10 where 10 is the highest), and sites used the tag to maintain their page ranks (or PR in short) even though they have to allow visitors to add their links. When the 'no follow' tag is enabled, your link back is only visual and search engines are not suppose to crawl the link and give it page ranks. The same method is used by bloggers to curtail the bleeding page rank effect of visitors' link, so before you post your comments and links (you aimed for the link) click on the view button to see their source code first, and if you see the no follow tag, you should ignore them as posting will be a waste of time. However, you can still find plenty of Forum and Blog sites that allowed a useful link back.

Pod casting

Pod casting is an old idea with a new name. Basically, it is the use of audio files to deliver a message and the reason it is getting popular is because people can download (usually an MP3 audio file) the pod cast unto their portable devices like Apple's Ipod so that it can be listened at a later time like when they are on their way driving to work. If you have a message (could be a joke or a sales pitch) for your visitors, you can embed it on your website or your Blogs and encourage your visitors to download it unto their computers for a listen. You could also add a short video file as videos are very popular now. Both audio and video pod casting is expected to get popular as a method of disseminating information in the future, if what is happening to websites like You Tube is of any measure. You can also download free University lectures from eminent professors and listen to it in your spare time. Why not sponsor such podcasts?

As an indication of what is going to happen in the future, cell phones, especially those of the sophisticated types are loaded with various video capabilities so that you can stream and download video files while on the move. As mobile broadband (3G) becomes available everywhere, video files (comparatively large) might be the in-thing, so preparing your Internet Marketing campaigns with video messages could be your best bet. Since most people have cell phones, it is good to postulate that people could just use 'voice command' to perform mobile search on their phones whilst on the move. This is where audio files will become important because with 'audio search engines', you can just yak on your command and get an audio result without looking at your mobile device! Hopefully, such a search engines will be available in the future (hopefully by 2010). However, an audio centric internet is another ball game, but one that is suitable for mobile users as they will not need to look at the web page. Presently, voice recognition computer programs are available, but it is still difficult to achieve 100 % accuracy, so we will have to wait for technology to catch up.

Press Releases

Press releases, especially those through the on-line Medias, can be a very cost effective way of driving traffic to your site. Releases that are fed through the prime syndicates have a large targeted group of people searching for news feeds. Newspaper and magazine editors troll the feeds from press release syndicates on a daily basis, even when they are on leave! They can't afford to miss any big news, right. Many trade newsletter editors are also getting in touch through automatic feeds from the news syndicates, and that is why getting your news out there is a cost effective way to get your self noticed. As you are allowed to have a link back to your site at the end of your press release statement, it will also tell the search engines the presence of your site so if you don't have anyone linking to you yet, this linking from the PR site will bounce you into the radar screen of the search engines. And since most major Media companies' site has a high page rank and is crawled by the search robots on an hourly basis, having this back link to your site is a boost to your linking program. Company matters and new product releases should be channeled to PR Medias for cost effective marketing efforts. Press releases are highly targeted so you should put up a budget for it as far as possible. It order to make full use of press releases, you will have to polish up your copy writing skills as only news worthy ones get read. Writing headlines is one thing, but writing good headlines that gets attention is another!

Social networks

Social network sites offer another avenue to place your links, but since the nature of such sites is geared towards social networking, you have to post your commercial links subtly so as not to be considered spamming. You could of course tell others what you do with your website, but thread cautiously. With more people using their mobile devices to connect to their social networks, you should have a mobile page that is specially designed to engage the smaller screens of cell phones. Social networks are getting more popular all the time and will encroach into everything that we do daily, so take sometime to formulate your various marketing around them. The possibilities with social networks are plenty, and here you will find a lot of other people's inputs, and suggestions that can spark new ideas and new approaches for your internet marketing. If you are thinking of a viral campaign, then look at social networks for nothing travel faster than all those people connected and talking at the same time! With cash endowed companies buying up social networking sites like MySpace and FaceBook, you can bet that they will stay current for some time.

Page Rank

Page rank is a Google invention and it is a ranking system for websites where ratings are given from a scale of 1 to 10, where 10 is the highest rate. It is shown on a small green pixel bar at the top of the browser with the Google Tool bar plug-in. Popular sites like MSN and Yahoo are rated around 9 whilst least popular and new sites might not get any ratings. In ranking each page, Google has to take into consideration of about a few hundred determinants which together makes up its propriety 'algorithms'. No body knows exactly what these variables are, but the general public usually right guessed it from the many webmasters postings which form the basis of SEO techniques.

It was a popular method to see who is rated higher than others and was used by webmasters to decide who to link to in their linking campaigns. The thinking then was that you would not seek links from sites that ranked lower than yours. If you were to install the Google 'tool bar' in your browser, you will be able to see what the website's (the one that is opened in your browser) page rank is and if it is high, you can then approach them to get a link.

At its peak, getting high PR was the main preoccupation of webmasters trying to benefit from the rating, so much so that some sites with high ratings took the opportunity to 'sell' their links to lesser sites. Later, Google, sensing the issue was getting out of hand, came out to disclaim the importance of PR and went out to change their algorithms to downgrade the PR issue in their SERP. As a result, it is not uncommon to see even sites with low PR (like 3 or 4) ranking above sites with higher PR (6 or 7) in the SERP listings. Search engines like Yahoo and MSN also have their own equivalents of PR and you can also install the Yahoo tool bar to check on Yahoo PR.

Looking ahead

It used to be through whisperings that people get the news to others, but it is more likely that the new viral message will be propagated through Instant Messaging (IM) or Short Messaging Services (SMS) using mobile phones. Another medium is the ever popular video format, and with the increasing availabilities of broadband and 3G mobile channels, videos might become the de facto medium for fast propagation of happenings. With changes in the way people accessing the internet, it is inevitable that Internet Marketing will also change. With more of the young generation becoming more mobile, there will also be more people looking and doing their things on the tiny screens, and from anywhere that has mobile services. How you can manage your marketing through such an environment will depend on how forward looking you are. What worked in 2005 might not work anymore! There are more mobile devices (about 2 billion at end of 2006) in the world now than desktop computers and their rate of increase is about 30 % per annum. At least 10% of those mobile users in developed countries did access the internet through their cell phones in 2006. The potentials in developing countries like China and India is even greater as there are less land lines there so people would be more than likely to access the internet through mobile devices, rather then fixed telephone access points.

Already, mobile searches have taken off and it will definitely impact on the way we conduct our marketing on the net. Internet Marketing as we know it is structured to draw buyers mostly through credit card payments, and in order for it to be viable, the value of each transaction should not be less than ten dollars, exclusive of shipping charges. But with the advent of Mobile Internet Marketing, we would have to take into cognizance of 'micro payments' methods that are more viable with the younger generations (including kids) whom normally don't have credit cards. Such payments may be less than a dollar's worth, but because there is bulk; the total amount of monetary transaction may exceed that from the normal types of transaction. Micro payment transactions will include low value purchases like cinema tickets, cigarettes and bottles of beer. It might not be viable to collect payments through the net then, so websites might have to find other functions, like acting as the main advertiser, drawing in customers, but directing them to the nearest outlets or retailers (with micro payment access points). In Japan and Korea, mobile phones are designed with chip sets that can do micro payments just by waving the handset close to a debit assessment point. This method might become popular because mobile devices have the capability of letting others know their locations from either using location based software or subscribing to location services from network providers. Advertising (web site based) might then take a totally new form as it would include the ability to track the whereabouts of potential customers, regardless of any privacy issues. Probably, people might be willing to trade some of their privacies while using mobile devices for some freebies paid by advertisers. Internet Marketing will take a whole new form then.

Chapter 4

BRANDING

Online Branding

The moment that you put up a web presence, you should begin to brand your company. Branding is a continuous exercise, and the main reason to brand something is to build up an image so that it will become a recognizable asset. For all your time and effort, you should be rewarded with a brand that is distinguishable, valuable and something that people feels proud to associate with. Branding exercise is a long journey and before you even begin, you will have to decide on how others view you. You will also have to be consistent and upfront about your type of brand, so that it would leave a good image about it in the people's mind. Your product, your quality, your service and your front desk will determine the kind of brand that others will remember you by.

I will now tell you what you can do with on-line branding. There are two things that you can do to improve your on-line presence.

First, make your website rank high in as many keyword terms as possible. This is a long term exercise and will demand a lot of hard work. Undisputedly, when your website ranks well in the SERP, you will automatically get more traffic. When your site ranked number one, people will subconsciously think that it is the best, even though your product might not be the best at all!

Second, when people keep seeing your brand popping up in their searches, they will subconsciously form an impression that your brand is associated with that keyword, even though they might not click on to find out more. This is not unlike the billboard advertisements that you see strewn along the motor highways. The more you see, the more it sinks in your subconscious mind, until you even see it in your dreams! When you see the advertisements, you might not even think of it, but it will somehow shape your thoughts after office hours. And when that particular keyword is triggered, the subconscious mind will recall back what they have seen many times before. They called it mind associations. And once it sticks, it doesn't get erased easily. Would you not like your brand to reach such a status? Have you not noticed that there are so many advertisements from the big boy brands on the net that you might think the internet turf belongs to them? But they are also paying big bucks for it though, and they can't stop paying, otherwise people might think they have folded up, so they are in a dilemma, sort of!

So how do you get high search rankings in multiple keywords? The trick is to have a lot of text in your website, but not too much to drown out your product. Let us just take an example.
Supposing you are selling flower pots and your page only consist of the text 'ABX Flower pot' and a fantastic picture of your product. Now, supposing the search engine found your site and list your page in its data servers. As listing are slotted into keyword categories, your site will be listed under keywords like 'ABX, ABX Flower, ABX pot, Flower pot', so your site only appear in four categories. Now, supposing you increase your text to 'ABX flower pots, your essential garden accessory'. If you do the math, there is now many more combination of words, including 'ABX Flower pots accessory'

and 'ABX Flower pots essential gardening accessory' and so on and so forth. You are now listed in many more keyword phrases and your chance of being found increases as your number of text increase. No text means you do not get listed at all! You get the point.

Are people now typing combination of keywords in their searches? Yes, more and more people are keying in multiple keywords now, sometimes even a whole query string consisting of a complete sentence. The main reason is that when they key in just two words, they get plenty of listings (sometimes in the millions) and surfers will have to spent a lot of time drilling on each link to see what the site is all about. In short, searching for something is a real time waster. They now prefer to key in more specific keywords just to get their search right the first time out. People are getting impatient at the amount of work that they have to perform drilling down the SERP just to get at wake answers. Well, those were the days when all you have to do is just keying in two letter words and you get good relevant results! I have to use opening and closing quotation marks now just to cut down the chaff and regain my internet session time!

So the way to go for your website is to put more text into your copy. I just love text and never cease to get surprised at the number of keyword combinations that turn up in the SERP. On a brighter side, there are new search sites that incorporate a little window that shows a brief graphic view of the site in the SERP. Viewing this little window (including a miniaturized graphics) will allow the surfer to determine whether it has the appropriate content. The downside of these search engines is that downloading will be slower, so those with slow internet connections will have to be patient.

Email Marketing

Most people would have been familiar with email marketing by now. Any one who has an email accounts would have received many emails, much of it unsolicited and are considered spam mails. Almost 95% of such spams are soliciting for you to buy this and buy that, and some of it even has virus contents, it is no wonder that email marketing has got itself a very bad connotation. There is no doubt that when email marketing is done well, it does a good job in enlightening people to the availability of new products and services. If you think that you have a very good product that you would like to introduce it to the people, by all means use email marketing to get your sales. You can get your own list of op-in email accounts from your own site or you can buy op-in list from marketers to send your offers to. Email marketing has been an effective marketing medium so far, but the big boys are not using it. It has to do with corporate image and if you do not want to be associated with spamming, then my best advice is not to use it. Maybe its prime time is over, so move on to better things. Good brands don't spam and good spammers don't brand!

Off-line Branding

We have been using off-line Medias for branding for a long time, but with the advent of the internet, these familiar channels like newspapers, magazines, radio, television and direct mails seems not to be attractive any more. Part of the reason has to be the cost and partly because it is very much easier to use on-line branding exercises. An inherent benefit of off-line Medias is that it can deliver an impact full awareness on a small local area and for new enterprises that need a good local support will do well to channel its branding exercise at the local area first before it expands to the international front. If however your product has an international potential, you can use special trade magazines to advertise your presence.

Besides using traditional Medias for branding, there are other activities that can bring in a lot of awareness for your company. There are many charitable functions that you can contribute. There are raffles and sport events that you can sponsor prizes to. In many instances, a small contribution can bring in plenty of goodwill. Schools and colleges are also places where you can contribute and small value prizes with the corporate name printed on them can bring about long lasting corporate brand awareness.

At the end of the day, if you have done a good job at branding, you would be rewarded with an asset that might worth a few million dollars. You can keep on building it, or if you seek retirement then sell off the asset. Either way, you would benefit from this great experience called Internet Marketing.

Chapter 5

Logistics

Most Internet Marketing companies started off in a small way and in many instances, logistical requirements consist of a small office with spaces for the storage of finished goods. Depending on the types of products that you deal with, there will also be a section that handles packaging and delivery of the finished products. Offices are usually sited away from city centers, but should not be too far away from the shipping companies. Packaging is an important aspect of Internet companies and should be efficient and in good taste. First impression is important, so your goods should be delivered in the best of attire.

Shipping

Where tangible products are concerned, shipping charges can become a critical part of your setup. If possible, always state the total shipping charges upfront on your website. Do not lure your customers to the check out section without telling them of the total amount that they have to pay. If you want to go far in your Internet Marketing exercise, please don't ever slap in those notorious 'hidden charges' as they will leave your customers with a bad taste and it is a bad way to do business.

Unfortunately, there are many internet companies that sell ordinary items that are available everywhere and because of small margins; they inevitably lure their customers with very low price offer for a start and pump up the shipping charges to make the whole thing profitable. Before you even design your web site, you have to check out the shipping charges for your products first. This is so critical especially when you have to ship the goods overseas, so make sure you have the figure before you put it in your check out counter. Some shopping carts have an automatic calculator to calculate the total shipping charges, but sometimes it might confuse your customers if the cart is too sophisticated. Internet buyers are more finicky than their brick and mortar cousins, and if your shopping cart is difficult to navigate, they might abandon the buy half way through.

Returns

Well, when you sell through the internet, you have to be prepared to accept returns. You should also have to be upfront on your returns policy and you should state very clearly of the terms on your website. Before your customers buy from you, they will most likely scrutinize your returns policy, just in case they find your product not acceptable. Having a clearly stated policy will give your buyers the much needed confidence where buying from the internet site is concerned. As returns will surely involve some shipping cost, clearly stating as to whom bears it is a good policy, otherwise disputes will arise. Such things may adversely tarnish your image and brand.

Payments

Choosing the right type of payment structure for your Internet Marketing is a critical part of the whole exercise. Get it wrong, and you will have nightmares. Generally, the types of on-line payment system that you will find in the market will depend on your locality. You should have a payment gateway that can accept the major credit cards like Visa, Master and American Express. If your bank offers you a merchant account, by all means accept it, and if not, then using a third party account is advisable. You will however have to weigh the cost first because it varies according to your overall transactions. When you begin your selling, it is most likely that you will not have many sales to talk about and therefore your cost per transaction will be high. In such cases, it might be more viable to use a low cost system like Pay Pall or Google's CheckOut for a start. Then there is the issue of 'chargeback' by credit card users, so you will have to prepare for it and reflect it in your product prices.

Besides the above mentioned payment methods, there are others like bank wire and check payments. These methods work on a slower basis, but at least it will not give rise to chargebacks. Some products are better handled by these later methods, but generally, customers want instant gratifications, so they normally prefer using credit cards. Then again there is the issue of credit card particulars getting stolen, so if you can, do allow the other slower methods of payments for more choices.

Chapter 6

Your Vision

You are reading this in the internet age and as there are no borders in this realm, you will need to have a vision that is appropriate for whatever that you do. Your vision must be a Global one, no less. After having read all the essential tips, you are now above many others, so I will expect nothing less than to make Your Brand go Global from you.

May you reach out to the skies and spread your visions among all of us. Please make us proud of you.

Thank you for being with me all this while.

yours sincerely,
Yap Tat Meng

Email: tmyapterry@gmail.com

Website: www.AirCoast.com

About the author:

Yap Tat Meng has been inventing for many years and in those many years of dreaming up ideas, he has always habored the wish to one day establish his very own brand. However it was a difficult dream to achieve because of the insurmountable obstacles and the heavy financial requirements that was not forthcoming.

Then came the Internet, and everything began to be a possibility again. He then took the opportunity to learn computer and got himself involved in putting up a website to sell his wares. There were a lot of learning for the new medium, but everything was worth it. That was in 2000, and today he has finally achieved his life long wish to sell his own branded product through his web site www.AirCoast.com

Realizing that there were many others who shared his vision, he went about putting those experiences in writing. This book is the result of that endeavor. As a person, he does not believe in those many hypes that are found in the internet about people making millions of dollars with very little effort, so he would like his many readers to not believe in them as well, but to put in a good day's work in order to reap the fruits of their endeavor. The author's other book entitled Inventing: The moment before the spark came is available at Lulu, Amazon and BarnsandNobel. ISBN:978-1-4303-1304-5

You can contact the author at tmyapterry@gmail.com for further consultations in case you find that your Internet Marketing effort is not going as planned. He will be always available at your service.

www.ingramcontent.com/pod-product-compliance
Lightning Source LLC
Chambersburg PA
CBHWC51212050326
40689CB00008B/1281